The Jarrold Book of

The Countryside in Spring

with text by **E. A. ELLIS**

Jarrold Colour Publications, Norwich

Although spring is apt to be a fickle season in these islands, with waves of warm and cold, dry and wet weather following one another in uncertain succession, the calendar of Nature follows a predetermined order linked to the lengthening of days and the overall increase in warmth once the vernal equinox has passed. A few hot days in April are enough to speed the blossoming of small winter annuals on sandy ground and to bring forth butterflies, bumble-bees, queen wasps, ladybirds and a great many other insects from hibernation. Hedgebanks become starred with early flowers, meadows bright with lady's-smocks, marsh marigolds and cowslips, and woodland dells filled with primroses and bluebells as the weeks go by. Wayside shrubs and trees burst into bloom and leaf, early or late according to the species. Many mosses of arid habitats perfect their fruiting and cease growth as the strength of the sunshine increases, but most kinds of ferns, lurking in moist and shady haunts, put forth their young fronds only when the risk of frost damaging them is past. Plant life embarks on its great annual competition for a place in the sun, with many dwarf species completing their work of growth and reproduction rapidly before they become overshaded by taller species, notably forest trees. We look for the appearance of familiar spring butterflies such as the orange-tip along the lanes and the holly blue in woods and gardens, and sometimes the first immigrant red admirals reach us from southern Europe before the end of May. As insects become more plentiful, spiders resume activity; especially noticeable are the various wolf spiders which hunt their prey and are seen running over the ground in open places such as sand dunes and banks of ditches when the sun shines. The young of some of the orb-spiders, spinners of geometric webs, hatch out in swarms from silken cocoons early in spring and disperse gradually, often behaving as little cannibals in the process. Many young snails and slugs emerge from eggs at this time, but the adults of some species, such as the vari-coloured banded snails, creep out of winter quarters to indulge in nuptial frolics soon after mild, moist weather has tempted them abroad in spring. Pond snails also become active and may be seen rising to the surface on sunny days when aquatic algae are seething with bubbles of oxygen. Frogs and toads gather at ponds for spawning and attract attention by their loud croaking choruses. Snakes and lizards come out to bask in the early sunshine and presently take part in strange courtship rituals. For many freshwater fishes spring is the breeding season. Some species gather in huge shoals for this purpose while others go off in pairs to seek separate territories. Smelts and lampreys come up rivers from the sea to spawn in spring, while flounders which have wintered in fresh waters return to salt. This is also the time when swarms of minute elvers enter the mouths of our rivers after journeying from the eels' breeding haunts in the depths of the Atlantic Ocean. While a great many birds which have wintered here depart for their northern homelands, we welcome the return of summer's swallows, cuckoos, warblers and a host of other birds from the far south. Sometimes the immigrants are held up by adverse winds or they may meet with a dismally cold reception on their arrival, but usually they lose no time before building nests and rearing young in their accustomed niches in the countryside, trusting in what the future will bring. More and more birds add their voices to the dawn chorus which reaches its peak towards the middle of May, when cuckoos and nightingales are most ardent and the crooning of turtle doves adds a late contribution to the music-making. This singing, so pleasing to our ears when we rise early enough in the morning to hear the full chorus, is the means used by cock birds for establishing and maintaining breeding territories which are defended fiercely when rivals of the same species venture within their boundaries. Nearly all birds look to provide their chicks with a high proportion of insect food at this season. For many species this need is supplied by the caterpillars feeding on young foliage as trees and bushes come into leaf. If it were not for this predation, vegetation would suffer much more damage. At the same time, insect life generally reaches abundance very quickly and in great variety everywhere as the weather becomes warmer. Gnats and mayflies rise from the waters, black St Mark's flies drift high in the air from the fields, aphids multiply in clusters on growing plants, wild bees come out of earth burrows to forage far and wide for nectar and pollen to store in freshly prepared nests. At night, numerous moths and cockchafer beetles take to the air, some to be snapped up by bats which are active from April onwards on all except the coldest nights. Many small mammals start breeding early in spring as more food becomes available and vegetation provides greater cover. Moles become very active, producing early litters of young. The earthworms which they pursue are also busy multiplying at this time and some of them build little cairns of stones over their holes as a means of keeping the soil moist in spring. The face of the countryside changes more speedily in some regions than in others in the course of spring, and this is only to be expected since the British Isles come within the influence of bleak winds on the east and north and the gentle warmth of south-westerly breezes on the Atlantic side. Day and night temperatures are more evenly balanced in the rainy west, where late spring frosts are exceptional, whereas in the dry eastern counties clear skies bring about a rapid heating of the land by day and as swift a chilling by night. As at other seasons, the sea everywhere modifies the coastal climate, while vegetation and wildlife generally respond differently in time at different altitudes. Since Gilbert White began to keep a record of the dates when certain plants came into leaf and blossom, birds sang, butterflies appeared and frogs spawned, similar phenological observations have been made by naturalists far and wide in Britain, and by this means it has become possible to compare the data in relation to the local climate on a broad scale. Within the main climatic zones revealed by this method, however, there are many interesting variations, and there can be little doubt that diaries of natural events in spring are well worth keeping year after year. Such records will help us to detect gradual overall trends of change in Britain's climate.

Hedgerows

As the days lengthen quickly after the spring equinox, wayside banks grow lush with verdure. Soon there are white stars of stitchwort, blue germander speedwell and glossy celandines brightening country lanes, with primroses tufting moist hollows and galaxies of dandelions opening on grass verges. Hedges are capped with the snow of blackthorn in April and fragrant May blossom later, while cow-parsley grows tall and crowned with the milk-white lace of its flowerets as the weeks go by, until the first wild roses open at the approach of summer. Various early butterflies appear in succession. In April we welcome the cuckoo, swallow and a host of other migrants. As hedges provide more leafy cover, more and more birds build nests in them, while small mammals also commence breeding activity.

1

1. BLACKBIRD (*Turdus merula*). Common in town and country, the blackbird has a melodious fluting voice, seldom heard before February, but often dominating the dawn chorus in April and May. The brown hen is usually responsible for building the nest, which consists of a basin-like structure of mud and litter with a slight grassy lining, placed in a tree, bush or outbuilding. The cock helps to feed the young. Favourite foods include earthworms, slugs and various soft fruits.

2. MOLE (*Talpa europaea*). Marvellously adapted for tunnelling in the earth, moles flourish in open country, gardens and woods almost everywhere. Hillocks of soil are thrown up at intervals when fresh runs are being made and larger mounds ('fortresses') are used for breeding. A single litter of two to six young is produced in a hidden nest of dead leaves in early spring. The young at first make shallow tunnels, often disturbing flower-beds. Earthworms are their chief food, collected as the animals travel round their extensive network of burrows roughly every four hours.

3. LONG-TAILED TIT (*Aegithalos caudatus*) **AT NEST.** These are our smallest titmice, spending most of their time flitting from tree to tree, collecting minute insects from the twigs. The nest is a beautiful domed structure of moss and lichen interwoven with spider silk and lined with a mass of feathers.

4. SWALLOW (*Hirundo rustica*). Our British swallows winter in South Africa and return each spring to nest mainly on beams inside buildings. Their twittering songs, long-pointed forked tails and touches of red round the beak distinguish them from martins. Two or three broods of young may be reared in a favourable season.

3

4

5

5. CUCKOO (*Cuculus canorus*). The cuckoo's voice is heard first each spring in late April and may continue until the first week in July. Only the male bird utters the familiar call, which may be answered by the bubbling cry of the female. The hen spends much of her time perched where she can observe the nesting activities of other birds, so as to judge when the moment is right for her to introduce her egg among those of the foster-parent. On hatching, the infant cuckoo heaves all other chicks and eggs out of the nest, so securing the whole attention of the fosterers. Cuckoos tend to return to the same places year after year and individuals usually parasitise the same species in whose nests they themselves were reared. Fewer hedgerow cuckoos are reared nowadays.

6. WREN (*Troglodytes troglodytes*). Wrens abound everywhere in our countryside and although many perish in cold winters the population recovers quickly through the rearing of numerous families. The polygamous cocks usually build several nests for the hens to choose from. These are bulky, domed masses of moss, bracken, dead leaves and grasses, hidden in thickets or clefts of rocks and walls.

7. DUNNOCK (*Prunella modularis*). Although commonly called the hedge sparrow, this common bird of hedgerows and gardens is easily distinguished by its slender beak with which it is able to pick up minute insects and spiders, usually from the ground or from tufts of moss. It flicks its wings jerkily as it moves around, uttering a loud 'seeping' note at intervals. The nest is usually hidden in a thick hedge.

6 7

8 

8. ORANGE TIP BUTTERFLY (*Anthocharis cardamines*). This single-brooded species is on the wing from April to early June. Only the male has orange patches on the wings, the female being white. Both are camouflaged by green and white mottling on the underside.

9. WALL BROWN (*Lasiommata megera*). Very much a sun-loving insect, this restless butterfly is common over much of England, the first brood appearing in May and the second in August. The green, pale-striped caterpillars feed on various grasses and are not easily noticed. The adult butterflies survive only briefly.

10

9

10. GERMANDER SPEEDWELL (*Veronica chamaedrys*). This brilliant blue 'bird's-eye' is conspicuous in short turf on verges and wayside banks from March to June. Single plants may spread widely and survive for many years. The flowers attract flies and bees, but remain open only briefly and tend to drop soon.

11. COW PARSLEY (*Anthriscus sylvestris*). The creamy white flowers of this common umbellifer, often called 'lady's lace', border English lanes almost everywhere in profusion during May. Before hedgerows existed, this plant grew chiefly along the edges of woods. The slender, parsnip-like roots have a nutty flavour.

12. DANDELION (*Taraxacum officinale*). Dandelions flower most plentifully in grassy places in April and May. They develop white, fluffy 'clocks' of seeds which have silken parachutes for wind-dispersal. The blooms open only by day, attracting many bees and butterflies. The somewhat bitter leaves can be used in salads and the roots may be roasted as a substitute for coffee.

13. MEADOW BUTTERCUP (*Ranunculus acris*). This tallest of the grassland buttercups flowers from May to July. It has deeply cut leaves and much-branched flower-heads. The blossoms attract many insects, including butterflies and small, metallic, day-flying moths. All buttercups contain acrid and somewhat poisonous juice and are usually avoided by grazing animals after trial.

14. COWSLIP (*Primula veris*). Still called 'paigles', their Anglo-Saxon name, in many places, the clustered, egg-yellow flowers are often gathered by country people for wine-making. They flourish mainly on chalk grassland, but much of this has been lost through ploughing in recent years. They are now restricted in some areas to grassy waysides, on soils rich in lime.

15. GREATER STITCHWORT (*Stellaria holostea*). The grassy leaves of this member of the chickweed family are inconspicuous, but the flowers have a startling beauty along hedgebanks from March to May. The plant thrives only in grassy habitats and is not a weed of cultivated ground. It has disappeared from many verges regularly polluted by motor traffic.

16. HAWTHORN (*Crataegus monogyna*). Bird-sown hawthorns are quick to form scrub on ungrazed open ground, but tend to be shaded out as trees overtop them in mature woodland. As planted shrubs they grow to perfection in hedges. The heavily scented flowers are attractive mainly to flies and beetles and their petals turn pink before falling, if days are sunny in early June.

14

15

16

17. COMMON CARDER BEE (*Bombus agrorum*). Seen here visiting a melancholy thistle, this universally common bumble-bee is active from April to September, visiting a wide range of flowers for nectar and pollen. Its long tongue enables it to obtain food from tubular flowers. It often colonises old nests of birds and mice. Pollen is stored in special pouches adjoining the brood-cells.

17

18. BROWN-LIPPED SNAIL (*Cepaea nemoralis*). Abundant along hedgebanks, in woods and on some sand dunes, this widespread species exhibits great variation in colouring and banding, being most commonly yellow in open habitats and predominantly red in shady haunts. It is a favourite food of song thrushes, which smash the shells on stones. When mating, these snails prick one another with 'Cupid's darts'.

19. CARDINAL BEETLE (*Pyrochroa serraticornis*). These brilliant scarlet insects with long, serrated antennae, may be seen in flight or crawling over leaves and flowers round the borders of woods chiefly in late May and June. Their elongate, yellowish-brown larvae have curiously flattened bodies adapted for living immediately under the bark of rotting tree trunks, especially elm.

20. ST MARK'S FLIES (*Bibio marci*). Swarms of these jet-black, hairy flies emerge from grassland and drift over the countryside in early May, where they are snapped up eagerly by newly arrived swifts. They are traditionally associated with St Mark's Eve (25 April) but allowance must be made for eleven days having been dropped from the English Calendar in 1752, making the expected time of emergence 6 May.

21

21. GREAT HORSETAIL (*Equisetum telmatiaea*). The elegant spore-bearing cones of this primitive plant may be found coming up in great numbers on wet, clayey land, usually near streams and ditches, in spring, accompanied by asparagus-like shoots which later expand to form forests of graceful feathery green fronds.

22. ST GEORGE'S MUSHROOM (*Tricholoma gambosum*). A pleasantly edible species appearing commonly on grassland, especially chalk pastures, from April to June. It has a creamy cap and stalk, crowded, wavy, brittle gills and white spores. In some places it forms large 'fairy rings'.

23. COMMON MOREL (*Morchella esculenta*). This is a near relative of cup-fungi, with a wrinkled stalk and irregularly honeycombed top and is found sprouting from bare soil under trees and hedges in April and May. It is commonest in chalk and limestone districts.

24

24. CUCKOO-SPIT. The white froth seen everywhere on the stems and shoots of a great variety of plants in late spring is produced by the young of froghoppers, which protect their soft bodies from desiccation by this moist covering, while they imbibe sap through their beaks. The adult hoppers move about freely.

Waterways and Marshes

The growth of aquatic plants is slow at the beginning of spring, except for blanket-forming algae and microscopic forms. In marshes and meadows, however, marsh marigolds, pussy willow catkins and lady's smocks brighten the scene quite early and gradually the greenery of sprouting reeds and sedges supersedes the pale gold and brown of winter's legacy of litter. Brimstone butterflies lay eggs on buds of buckthorn. Numerous moths flock to the sallow bloom at night. In East Anglia the lordly swallow-tail swoops over the fens towards the end of May. From April onwards the number of dragonflies and other insects with aquatic larvae increases. Spring is the main spawning season of most of our freshwater fishes as it is for the amphibians, while swamps and reed beds become lively with chattering warblers.

25. SNIPE (*Gallinago gallinago*). Nesting in damp, rushy places, snipe draw attention to their presence in early spring by their swift circling and 'drumming' overhead. The sound can be mistaken for the bleating of goats and is produced by vibrations of the outer tail feathers as the birds make their steep descents. They are commonly double-brooded. The very long bill has a sensitive tip which comes into play as they probe boggy ground in search of worms and insect larvae.

26. OTTER (*Lutra lutra*). Although otters have vanished from many of their old haunts in recent years, they are still present in most of our river valleys, but are seldom encountered except when they are fishing in streams at night.

27. HERON (*Ardea cinerea*). The gaunt grey heron or 'harnser' is a familiar sight, standing at the waterside in wait for fishy prey. Its massive twiggy nests are built in tree-tops, especially alders, often colonially, and the young are fledged by late May.

28. GREAT CRESTED GREBE (*Podiceps cristatus*). Once rare, but now widespread on our lakes as the result of strict protection, this largest of our grebes builds floating nests of reedy litter. The fluffy chicks are often to be seen riding pick-a-back.

26

27

28

29. SWALLOWTAIL BUTTERFLY (*Papilio machaon*). The native race of this magnificent insect remains indigenous only to the fens surrounding the Norfolk Broads nowadays, where its green and black caterpillars feed almost exclusively on milk parsley which abounds there. The butterflies can be seen flying swiftly over the marshes on sunny days, chiefly from late May to early July. They are wide-ranging in their search for flowers and often visit local village gardens, but are perhaps most attracted by the magenta blossoms of ragged robin (see opposite page). The caterpillars pupate in early summer, the chrysalids being attached by silken loops to various marsh plants. Varying numbers of them produce an autumn brood of butterflies, but usually most remain dormant until the following spring. Some of the larvae succumb to the attacks of parasitic insects and occasionally they are taken by jays, but they feed in the open and their warning colours protect them from most predators. When disturbed, they expose a pink forked organ over the head and emit a pineapple scent. Very occasionally black and smoky butterflies appear in the population. Examples of the typical Continental form widespread on the European mainland turn up occasionally as immigrants.

30. RAGGED ROBIN (*Lychnis floscuculi*). This bright-pink marsh campion with finely divided petals flowers most freely where clearings have been made in the previous season. It needs good illumination and space to grow to perfection. The blossoms appear from May to July and attract many insects, including bumblebees and, in Norfolk, round the Broads, swallowtail butterflies.

9

31

32

33

34

31. SNAKE'S-HEAD (*Fritillaria meleagris*). These purple or occasionally milk-white chequered lilies used to flourish on many water-meadows in south and east England, but are now uncommon since there is less permanent pasture land. Blooming at the end of April, they persist most successfully where meadows are mown or grazed after the plants have shed seed in early summer. This treatment prevents overshading by taller and more aggressive forms of vegetation.

32. COMMON OSIER (*Salix viminalis*). This most popular of osiers used in basket-making has long, pliant stems produced as the result of pollarding stocks close to the ground. As in all willows, male and female catkins develop on separate trees early in spring and yield abundant nectar which attracts bees and butterflies. Later, the female trees scatter quantities of fluffy seeds which colonise bare mud, such as that of river dredgings.

33. WATER FORGET-ME-NOT (*Myosotis scorpioides*). This is the plant to which the name 'forget-me-not' was first given. It is a very common perennial herb of watersides and the wetter parts of marshes and often forms extensive carpets in swampy thickets, such as the alder- and sallow-carrs of East Anglia. It flowers from May onwards through the summer. Like its relatives, it used to be known as 'scorpion-grass' from the resemblance of the coiled flower-heads to the recurved tail of a scorpion.

34. LADY'S SMOCK (*Cardamine pratensis*). Also called 'cuckoo-flower' because it comes into bloom just as cuckoos are due in spring. It grows most plentifully in meadows which are lightly grazed or mown for hay in summer. The cress-like leaves can be eaten in salads and are a favourite food of the caterpillars of orange tip butterflies. New plants often arise from single leaflets which have been broken off. 'Double' flowers are fairly common in this species, also a white variety.

35. ROYAL FERN (*Osmunda regalis*). An old English name for this giant deciduous 'flowering' fern was 'Osmond the waterman'. It is a long-lived species growing in massive clumps in boggy places, often in the shade of alders. The sporangia are borne on distinct fertile, non-leafy fronds.

36

38

37

36. WATER CROWFOOT (*Ranunculus heterophyllus*). This is one of several small white buttercups found growing in ponds, ditches and streams. The massed blossoms sometimes look like snow-drifts. In this species the submerged leaves are finely divided and fennel-like, but those floating on the surface are kidney-shaped.

37. YELLOW FLAG (*Iris pseudacorus*). This wild iris grows in marshes and by pools and streams throughout Britain. It flowers most freely where the plants are exposed to plenty of light; in shady places only the sword-like leaves develop year after year. Fleshy sausage-shaped rhizomes spread just beneath the surface.

38. PALMATE NEWT (*Triturus helveticus*). The male in colourful breeding attire is shown here; the female lacks a crest on the back. This is mainly an upland species in Britain, entering pools to breed in March and emerging from the water by mid-June. The thread-like appendage at the tip of the tail distinguishes it.

39

39. GREAT CRESTED or WARTY NEWT (*Triturus cristatus*). The largest of our three British newts, this species appears almost black out of the water and has a warty skin. It is fairly common and widespread in and around lowland ponds. In spring, Newts lay eggs singly in folded leaves of various aquatic plants.

40. FROG SPAWN and TADPOLES. The spawn of the common frog is laid in jelly-like masses in March, whereas toad spawn is laid (rather later) in long ribbons. Frog tadpoles become freckled with gold and have long pointed tails while those of the common toad remain almost black above.

41. COMMON FROG (*Rana temporaria*). Very variable in colour, this is still our commonest and most widespread amphibian, although it has disappeared from many of its old haunts since certain pesticides and weed-killers have contaminated the countryside.

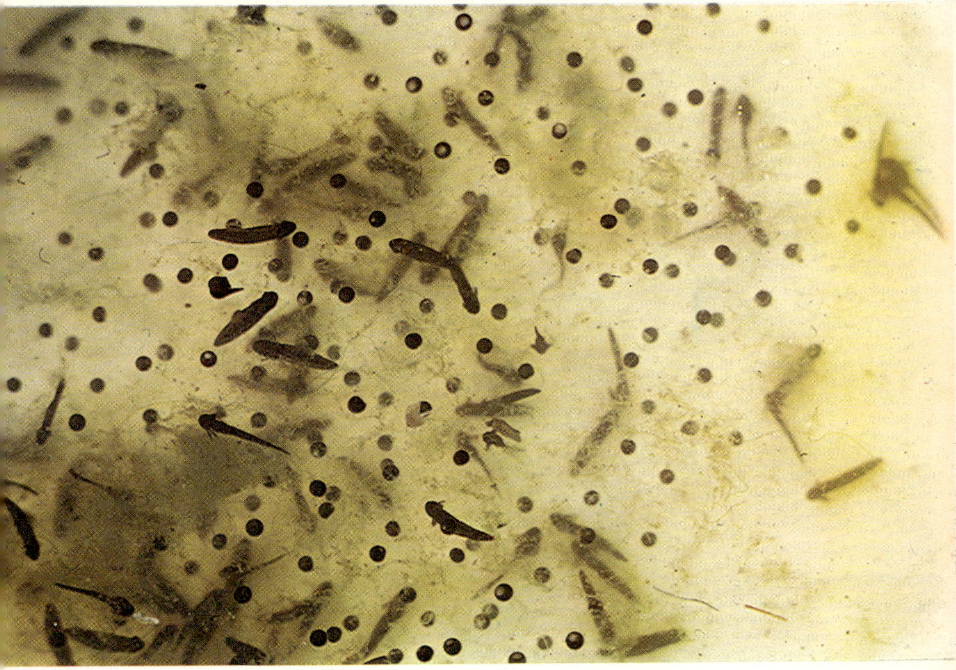

42. SWAMP SPIDER (*Dolomedes plantarius*). This is the rarer of our two large swamp spiders living in tall vegetation fringing boggy pools, being apparently restricted to one river valley in Suffolk. The other, *D. fimbriatus*, occurs in the New Forest and south-west Ireland. They dash out over the water to seize their prey.

43. ALDER-FLY (*Sialis lutaria*). These smoky-brown insects with black-veined wings may be seen flying clumsily or running over waterside vegetation on sunny days from April to June. Clusters of eggs are laid on leaves and twigs overhanging the water. The larvae are aquatic, living like miniature dragons.

44. REED BEETLE (*Donacia semicuprea*). The larvae of various metallic reed beetles feed on submerged rootstocks of marsh and water plants and obtain their air supply by tapping the tissues of these plants under water. The beetles emerge in late spring to fly in the sunshine and nibble leaves and flowers.

42

45

45. SEDGE CUP (*Sclerotinia sulcata*). The stalked cups (apothecia) of this fungus sprout from black, lengthwise-ribbed, spindle-shaped sclerotia embedded within the stalks of sedges (mainly tussock-sedges) in marshy places in spring. They liberate spores which infect the young flowering stems, which then die back from the top, rendering the flowers sterile. Conidial bodies develop on the bleached tissues and sclerotia renew growth in April.

46

46. CATKIN CUP (*Ciboria amentacea*). These often very long-stemmed apothecia shaped like wine-glasses can be found very commonly under alders and sallows in early spring. A careful search will show that they arise from the previous year's fallen male catkins of these trees, which have been preserved by the fungi in a mummified condition for their own use. When disturbed, they emit clouds of spores like mist and these infect the new crop of fallen catkins.

47

47. POPLAR AGROCYBE (*Agrocybe cylindracea*). Large clusters of this agaric may be seen sprouting from long-dead stumps and fallen trunks of black poplars and sometimes elms in spring. Their caps are at first pale tawny and slightly viscid when moist, but bleach on drying and become wrinkled and cracked in a distinctive manner. There is a white ring, often folded back, on the stalk. The crowded gills become pale brown at maturity and shed reddish-brown spores.

48. BARK 'PUFFBALL' (*Reticularia lycoperdon*). Many people are mystified by the appearance of soft milk-white excrescences on dead trunks of willow, alder and birch, and sometimes on old gateposts in early spring. These are more or less bun-shaped and soon develop a shining silvery skin on the surface. When ripe, they gradually peel and disintegrate as a mass of dark-brown, dry, powdery spores, like those of puffballs. They are the fruit-bodies of one of the larger slime-fungi (Myxomycetes).

49

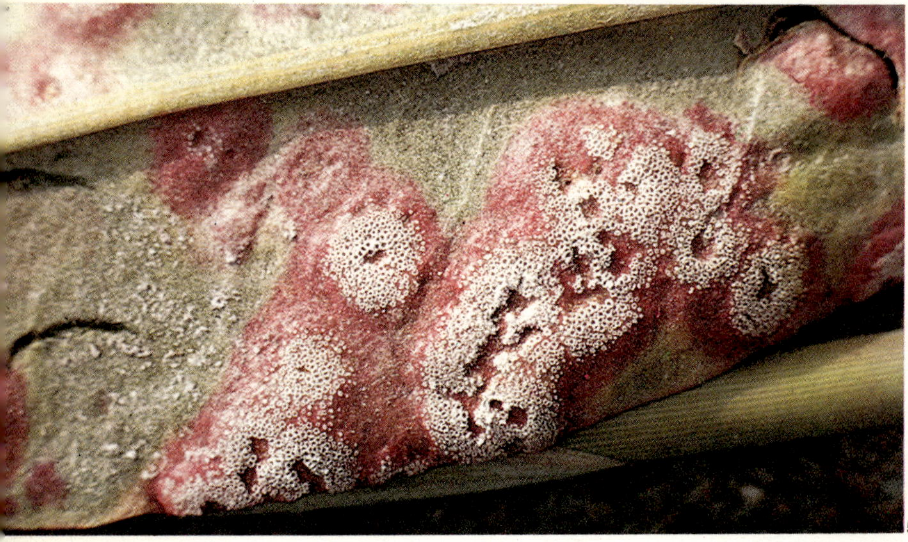

50

49. MARSH MARIGOLD RUST (*Puccinia calthaecola*). The whole life-cycle of this parasitic fungus is spent on the same host-plant. Our illustration shows the yellow clustercups (aecidia) appearing in spring, and small brown uredo-sori developing where aecidiospores have infected a young leaf.

50. REED RUST (*Puccinia phragmitis*). Docks growing in marshes develop crimson stains on their leaves in May and June. On the under-side they will be found honey-combed with white clustercups. Spores from these infect the young leaves of common reed, which then produce uredospores and teleutospores.

Coast

Just as in winter the sea has a softening influence on the coastal climate, so, as the sun's returning warmth comes to the countryside in spring, cool sea breezes tend to have a slightly retarding effect on vegetation near the coast, although lessening the risk of damage from frost on clear nights. Quite early we look for white drifts of blossoming scurvy-grass on the saltings, followed by the pink of thrift; but seashore vegetation on the whole blooms later in the year. April sees the awakening of lizards, adders and natterjack toads from winter lethargy in the dunes. Sea birds now flock to the cliffs and sand-spits all round our coast, bringing excitement and beauty to their traditional breeding-haunts with their wheeling flight and their screaming and whistling. A few butterflies haunt cliff slopes and dunes in May.

51. PUFFINS (*Fratercula arctica*). These small auks, appropriately called 'sea parrots' from their gaily coloured bill-sheaths developed in the breeding season, spend most of the year well out to sea, where they pursue small fish after the manner of penguins, using their wings under water. They return to coastal cliffs in early spring, assembling in large colonies for nesting. For this purpose most of them use burrows in turf on the slopes and cliff crests. Only a single white egg is laid.

52

52. COMMON GUILLEMOTS (*Uria aalge*). Very large numbers of these birds live in the seas round Britain. They begin to gather at their breeding-haunts on ledges of rocky cliffs early in the year, and in spring each hen lays a single large, spotted and scribbled, pear-shaped egg which she incubates precariously in due course. The shape of the egg prevents it from rolling off its rocky perch.

53. SEA CAMPION with SMUT (*Ustilago violacea*). The anthers of many campions and their near relatives are commonly parasitised by this smut-fungus, whose purplish-brown powdery spores are produced in place of pollen. The affected flowers often appear dark and dusty in their centres where the spores are scattered by rain or visiting insects. The fungus has a permanent base in the plant.

54. THRIFT (*Armeria maritima*). Tufts of sea pinks grow in great profusion on rocky cliffs and carpet the higher parts of salt-marshes with rosy, honey-scented blossoms in May and June. After flowering, the papery seed-heads persist for some months. Where the climate is mild, the cushions of finely grassy leaves remain green almost all the year, but on bleak coasts they wither in winter.

55. ENGLISH STONECROP (*Sedum anglicum*). This dwarf rock-plant forms spreading mats and cushions on ledges of sea cliffs and mountains and is often plentiful on sandy dunes and beach shingle, especially in the west of Britain. It grows best on acid rocks, avoiding chalk and limestone. The fleshy leaves are pale blue-green up to the time of flowering and then become tinged with red.

56

57

58

56. LONG-LEAVED SCURVY-GRASS (*Cochlearia anglica*). Common in south and east England, this is the lushest of the several scurvy-grasses producing conspicuous white flowers round the edges of muddy salt-marshes in early spring. These fleshy-leaved plants flourish on Arctic islands, where they used to be gathered and eaten by mariners as a protection against scurvy.

57. SPRING SQUILL (*Scilla verna*). Patches of this brightly coloured miniature bluebell bring enchantment to dry, grassy cliff-slopes in early spring. They are to be seen plentifully along some parts of our west coast and only scantily elsewhere, surviving chiefly in the more inaccessible places which escape trampling by summer's crowds of holiday-makers.

58. ALEXANDERS (*Smyrnium olusatrum*). This yellow-green umbellifer, coarse and celery-like, is conspicuous along road-verges round our coast and occasionally inland. It was known anciently as 'alisander' or 'olus-atrum', the black pot-herb, from the black seeds used as flavouring for meats and soups. Monks cultivated it in the Middle Ages, blanching the crowns like celery.

59. COMMON LIZARD (*Lacerta vivipara*). This lively, harmless reptile is found in every part of the British Isles, including Ireland. Although it likes to bask in the sunshine in dry, grassy and heathery places, snapping up an occasional insect, it also requires moist, shady retreats. The eggs are incubated within the mother's body up to the moment of hatching

60. COMMON TOAD (*Bufo bufo*). Except in the breeding season, this amphibian frequents dry places, burrowing into sandy soil by day and emerging mainly at night to hunt for worms, slugs and beetles. Whereas frogs take long leaps, these toads crawl and hop in a clumsy fashion. Their skins secrete an irritant fluid which acts as a deterrent to some enemies.

61

62

61. NATTERJACK (*Bufo calamita*). Also known as the 'running toad' from its habit of scuttling along like a mouse in the dusk, this species can be recognised by the light-yellow line running down the middle of its back and by its glittering emerald eyes. Once locally abundant in sandy places in many parts of Britain it is now relatively rare and protected by law where it breeds in temporary pools of dune hollows, chiefly on the coasts of East Anglia and Lancashire.

62. NATTERJACKS' BREEDING-POOL. This rain-filled hollow in a Norfolk dune-slack is a natural spawning site for natterjacks which live in the nearby sand-hills. It is quite shallow, with tufts of rush, moss and creeping willow growing in it. The toads arrive to mate and spawn there in April or May, but quite often their efforts come to nought through the pool drying out in the heat of June before the tadpoles have completed their development. Now conservationists provide deeper pools.

Woodlands

In woodland habitats, more than any other, plant life is swift to welcome the returning sun in spring, and to produce a wealth of foliage and blossom before the trees have come into full leaf and cast a deep shade. The ground becomes carpeted with pale wind-flowers, primroses and bluebells in rapid succession, before the end of May. They provide early refreshment for newly active insects, including butterflies and bees. The woods are filled with songs of birds at dawn and nightfall, reaching their greatest volume by mid-May, as native species are joined by fresh waves of incoming migrants week by week. At this time also, there is a sudden increase in the mammal population as many species bring litters into the world, including squirrels in their snug tree-top nests and foxes in their 'earths'.

63

63. WILLOW-WARBLER (*Phylloscopus trochilus*). This is the smallest and by far the most common and widespread of the leaf-warblers coming to Britain for the spring and summer months. Its sweet little bursts of quick-running notes, fading to a whisper at the end, can be heard almost everywhere in deciduous woodlands from mid-April to June. The somewhat domed nest is nearly always built at ground level in a litter of dead leaves and twigs, presently concealed by new undergrowth.

64

64. YOUNG SONG THRUSH (*Turdus philomelos*). The speckled thrush delights us with its singing from the tree-tops in town and country alike for more than half the year, from January onwards, but especially when nesting is at its peak in April and May. Two or three families may be reared. The nestlings look rather fierce and reptilian.

65. COCK BLACK-CAP (*Sylvia atricapilla*) **FEEDING CHICKS.** Numerous black-caps arrive here from the Mediterranean region in early spring to nest mainly in tall shrubs and brambles in woods. The hen has a rusty-brown cap. The song is very loud, silvery and melodious, with intermittent churring.

66. HOLLY BLUE (*Celastrina argiolus*). Butterflies emerging from overwintered chrysalids in spring commonly lay eggs on the flowers of holly towards the end of May. The population of this species fluctuates between the extremes of scarcity and abundance over the years across much of our countryside.

67. HOLLY BLUE CATERPILLAR. The spring brood of these pale-green, slug-shaped larvae is reared chiefly on the young fruits of holly, although flowers of several other woodland shrubs provide a substitute at times. Butterflies produced from these lay their eggs on ivy buds.

68

69

68. WOOD DOG VIOLET (*Viola riviniana*). This is the most widespread scentless violet to be found blooming with primroses in our woods, on shady hedgebanks and grassy mountain slopes. The flowers are of a bluish-violet colour, with pale, rather thick, up-tilted spurs and conspicuous appendages on the sepals. The plants have rosettes of broadly heart-shaped, pointed leaves and often produce a wealth of blossoms from April to June.

69. MOSCHATEL (*Adoxa moschatellina*). Carpeting sandy woodland soils, with its light-green foliage and even paler-green flower-heads in spring, this small plant is apt to be overlooked, even when in full bloom, at bluebell time. The flower-heads have four faces and for this reason are sometimes called 'town-hall clocks'. The name Moschatel comes from the plant's musky fragrance.

70. CUCKOO-PINT (*Arum maculatum*). Also known commonly as 'lords and ladies', this greenish wild arum with shining, arrow-shaped leaves (often spotted with purple) comes into bloom in April. The leaves die down by the end of June, leaving cylindrical spikes of berries, which become orange-scarlet when ripe. Small flies are attracted by the foetid scent of the flowers and are imprisoned overnight in traps, being released later after they have become dusted with pollen.

71. BLUEBELL (*Endymion nonscriptus*). Bluebells carpeting the woods in May and June provide one of the chief delights of our countryside. Usually it takes several centuries for a wealth of the flowers to reach perfection as seen in some ancient oak and beech woods. Picking the blooms does little harm in itself, but excessive trampling of the leaves is very damaging, since it is these which have to manufacture the food which goes into the bulbs for the next year's growth. The plants die down in summer, after expelling shiny, black seeds. The slender, drooping bells, though mostly blue, are occasionally white or lilac-coloured. The sturdier Spanish Bluebell with more open flowers is commonly naturalised.

71

72

73

72. WILD DAFFODIL (*Narcissus pseudonarcissus*). England's dwarf native daffodils, known also as Lent lilies or crowbells, flourish in open woods and moist grassland, chiefly in the west and south. The flowers come very early in spring.

73. BEECH (*Fagus sylvatica*). The male flowers of beech are conspicuous in May among the young, light-green foliage. They shed clouds of pollen with every puff of wind. The trees seldom bear nuts until they are at least fifty years old.

74. PRIMROSE (*Primula vulgaris*). In the western parts of Britain where the climate is moist, primroses flourish freely on wayside banks and in the open countryside; but in the eastern counties, mainly in damp woods.

75

75. MALE FERN (*Dryopteris filix-mas*). The young gold-green fronds of this very common and widespread fern uncurl and contribute much to the beauty of the woodland undergrowth at bluebell time. In those parts of Britain which experience mild, damp winters, the old fronds often remain green almost up to the time when the new year's growth begins in May. This fern grows rather stiffly erect at an angle which ensures that any dead leaves showered down by trees will be shuffled off with the slightest movement of air, so the fronds remain fully exposed to the naturally sparse illumination available in woodlands.

76. COMMON COCKCHAFER (*Melolontha melolontha*). Also frequently called the 'May-bug' and 'blind bee', this beetle sometimes appears in very large numbers in late May and June. By day it lurks in the undergrowth, but emerges at dusk to fly clumsily round tree-tops and other tall objects. These mass flights are for mating, but the insects also settle on trees and devour leaves. Eventually the females retire to the ground, where they insert eggs in the soil. These produce half-curled, plump, creamy grubs which feed on various roots for the next three or four years before developing into fully-fledged beetles.

77. GRASS or RINGED SNAKE (*Natrix natrix*). The yellow and black collar identifies this harmless snake. Growing up to four feet long, it inhabits wooded and marshy country throughout England and Wales, but not Scotland or Ireland. It climbs trees and takes to water in pursuit of fish and tadpoles. Prey includes frogs, small mammals and young birds. Hibernating underground, it emerges to bask and mate on sunny days in early spring. Clusters of white-skinned eggs are laid under rotting leaves and often in manure heaps in June and July, and the warmth of the decaying material assists incubation. The eggs hatch in autumn.

76

78. OAK-APPLE (*Biorhiza pallida*). The rosy-cheeked 'false apples' adorning green boughs of oak at the end of May are produced by the grubs of a gall-wasp. Their development begins after wingless female insects have climbed the trees to lay eggs in the oak buds earlier in the year. Presently the 'apples' fall; winged male and female insects emerge and eggs inserted in oak rootlets just underground produce a crop of scaly root-galls.

79. SULPHUR POLYPORE (*Laetiporus sulphureus*). The orange- and sulphur-yellow fruiting brackets of this rather soft woody fungus sprout very quickly from dead and dying trunks of many trees in spring, some specimens measuring 40 cm (almost 16 in.) across. Trees commonly attacked include willow, poplar and oak. Spores infecting wounds on healthy trees produce a mycelium which gives rise to decay within. The rot proceeds slowly.

80. CURRANT GALLS ON MALE CATKINS OF OAK. These develop in May after parthenogenetic female gall-wasps (*Neuroterus quercus-baccarum*) from the previous summer's common spangle galls on oak leaves have laid eggs in the flower buds. The 'currants' are at first translucent green and become flushed or speckled with red at maturity. Wasps of the bi-sexual generation emerge in June. The females fly to the trees and lay eggs in the undersides of oak leaves, giving rise to spangle galls.

81. POPLAR RUST (*Melampsora populnea*). The orange-yellow aecidial stage of this fungus is shown here on leaves of dog's mercury. It occurs commonly on this host in spring, while in other biological races of the same rust aecidia can be found developing on needles of European larch and on some of the pines. Later in the year the fungus goes on to attack aspen and white poplar, first producing small, orange-coloured powdery sori of uredospores and then teleutospores.

82

83

84

82. HALF-FREE MOREL (*Mitrophora semilibera*). This fleshy ascomycete sprouts from the black soil of damp woodlands early in May. It is often plentiful under poplars and on bare ground at the sides of old clay pits overgrown by hawthorns. Distinguished from other morels by the free margin of the small, conical cap, it varies greatly in size, as is seen in the illustration. The hollow stalk may be cylindrical or bulging either above or below, and is at first white and covered with mealy granules. The spore-bearing cap is yellowish brown with crinkled black ribs. The fungus is safely edible when cooked.

83. OVOID ARCYRIA (*Arcyria ferruginea*). This is one of the commoner slime moulds (Myxomycetes or Mycetozoa), with brightly tinted sporangia developing on the surface of rotten wood. There are other species of *Arcyria* with grey, buff, pink, red and pale-green fruit-bodies, consisting of spores mingled with elastic threads which are ornamented with little cogs, spines and ring-like thickenings, covered with a slight membrane which disintegrates, allowing the contents to disperse in powder and fluff. In a moist environment the spores produce swimming cells which multiply and produce sex-cells which form mobile protoplasm.

84. ANTLER SLIME-MOULD (*Ceratiomyxa fruticulosa*). In most of the slime moulds the spores are produced within the walls of the fruit-body (sporangium). *Ceratiomyxa* alone differs in bearing its spores externally on little threads projecting from the surface of forked, antler-like sporophores. These may be found sprouting on wet, rotten wood, following showery weather in spring and summer. They are very soft and fragile and usually white or cream-coloured, though occasionally of a yellow, apricot or pinkish shade. The process of reproduction, growth and feeding is of the same order as those found in other organisms of this group.

Moors and Heaths

Except for the vivid green of their bog-mosses, moorlands continue to appear bleak and sere in early spring, while the drier heaths are still patched with the rust of massed bracken fronds and bleached heather. But in due course the rosy bells of bilberry grace the fells, and the turf becomes streaked and splashed with the rainbow tints of milkwort, while cotton-sedges fill hollows with fluffy tops as bright as snow. Now we hear the bubbling music of curlews on home ground and, on some favoured stony heaths in the east, stone-curlews trill as wildly in the dusk, while nightjars purr among the scattered pines and birches. Soon the heaths are aglow with gorse blossom where wheatears and whinchats are tripping from rock to rock and bush to bush. On sunny days lizards and adders emerge to bask and mate.

85

85. WHINCHAT (*Saxicola rubetra*). After wintering in the warm south, this small relative of the robin appears in spring to frequent our heaths and dry brackeny places, most commonly in the northern and western parts of Britain. It has a habit of flicking its wings and tail all the time when perching on bushes, and utters short, rather metallic, 'chacking' call-notes. The male is darker and more richly coloured than the female shown here with young in her low, grassy nest.

86

86. GOLDEN PLOVER (*Pluvialis apricaria*). Breeding freely on many of our upland moors and more widely dispersed during the rest of the year, when they often assemble in large flocks, these beautiful waders attract notice by their clear, flute-like voices.

87. STONE CURLEW (*Burhinus oedicnemus*). Also known as the 'thick-knee' and 'Norfolk plover', this species is a summer visitor in small numbers to open tracts of heathland and stony fields in parts of East Anglia and southern England. The large golden eye is a distinctive feature. The two eggs are laid in rough scrapes.

88. NIGHTJAR (*Caprimulgus europaeus*). This owl-like, long-winged, perfectly camouflaged summer visitor to our heaths and open woodlands roosts by day and hawks moths at night. Active at dusk, it utters rhythmic purring notes.

89. WHEATEAR (*Oenanthe oenanthe*). These summer visitors frequent grassy heaths and open country generally, nesting in rocky crevices and rabbit burrows. The cock has a pale-grey back, while the hen is brown above, both having a conspicuous white rump. They frequently jerk their tails up and down.

90

91

90. EMPEROR MOTHS (*Saturnia pavonia*). These large silk-moths emerge from cocoons in April. The smaller male has orange colouring on the hind wings and feathery antennae and is able to find a mate by scent over long distances. The caterpillars are green with black bands and golden, bristly warts.

91. GREEN HAIRSTREAK (*Callophrys rubi*). Apart from the holly blue, this is our only small butterfly appearing on the wing as early as April. It may be seen fluttering about bushy spots on moors and heaths, the wings being blackish above and vivid green beneath. The caterpillars feed on gorse, broom, bilberry, bramble and dogwood.

92. WOOD ANEMONE (*Anemone nemorosa*). This common 'wind-flower', which typically carpets deciduous woodlands from the end of March to May, is seen here starring a patch of urn moss on open boggy ground fringing a Lakeland tarn. It can also be met with at heights of over 3,000 feet on some of the Scottish mountains.

93. HARE'S-TAIL COTTON SEDGE (*Eriophorum vaginatum*). Shown here at the flowering stage, this bristle-leaved plant of moorland bogs in areas of high rainfall develops conspicuous white fluffy seed-heads in late spring. It is a prominent feature of our larger stretches of moorland in north England and Scotland.

94

94. BILBERRY (*Vaccinium myrtillus*). Also known as whortleberry, whinberry and blaeberry, this deciduous moorland shrub is common over most of Britain, excluding East Anglia. The flowers may be found from May to July and the blue-black berries ripen in autumn, when they are commonly gathered for making jam.

95. BROOM (*Sarothamnus scoparius*). Common in dry, sandy places on lime-free soils, broom comes into bloom in late May, following the gorse. Its brushy green twigs do much of the work of photosynthesis normally the function of leaves. The blossoms do not secrete nectar, but are visited by bees for their pollen.

96

96. BOG VIOLET (*Viola palustris*). Common and widespread in acid bogs and marshes, especially in the west and north of Britain where rainfall is heaviest, but less frequent in our drier eastern counties, this violet has pale-lilac blossoms with dark veins and a blunt spur. The glossy, kidney-shaped leaves are normally rounded at the tip, but the sub-species *juressi* with pointed leaves occurs in some places. A succession of flowers appears from late April till early July, these being developed most freely in well-lit situations. Extensive patches of leafy plants without flowers are sometimes present in the shade of alders.

97

97. HAWTHORN and GORSE. England's remaining tracts of heathy common land are a delight in May when gorse and hawthorn are in full bloom. Such places are often haunts of the nightingale, linnet, yellow-hammer and sometimes the now uncommon red-backed shrike. They provide a refuge for isolated colonies of heath and grassland butterflies threatened elsewhere by agricultural development, and produce a succession of interesting grasses and wild flowers. There one may find lizards and slow-worms basking in the sunshine and tiger-beetles running over the sand, while the scented blossoms teem with bees and other insects all day.

98

98. BRACKEN (*Pteridium aquilinum*). The delicate light-green young fronds of bracken unfurl each spring in response to increasing warmth and sunlight, emerging from the bleached, rusty litter of the previous year's foliage. The presence of this cover is important for them when they first emerge, as it affords some protection from late frosts. Where the fern grows on open heaths the young shoots are often killed by frost. In East Anglia's arid Breckland region one finds 'frost pockets' in hollows devoid of bracken, from this cause. The ferns grow most vigorously year after year where the spring climate is more kindly.

100

99. HEATH LOUSEWORT (*Pedicularis sylvatica*). Unlike the tall red rattle, common in wet meadows, this is a low-creeping perennial frequenting boggy places. Its clusters of brilliant pink flowers and small, yellow-green, fern-like leaves are conspicuous in spring on the black peat and mossy cushions of the moors.

100. JUNIPER (*Juniperus communis*). This evergreen shrub flourishes on some English chalk downs, rocky slopes of the Lakeland fells and parts of the Scottish Highlands. The bushes seldom attain a height of more than fifteen feet, while many have a low-growing, flattened form. The male and female flowers develop on separate plants in spring.

101. JUNIPER RUST (*Gymnosporangium clavariiforme*). The boughs of many juniper bushes appear swollen in places and after rainy weather in spring the swellings increase and their surfaces erupt with soft, orange-yellow spikes which are the massed teleutospores of a rust-fungus. These spores germinate and the fungus produces orange clustercups on hawthorn leaves.

102. SMALL GARDEN BUMBLE-BEE (*Bombus hortorum*). This is one of the long-tongued species able to extract nectar from tubular flowers, especially those of red clover. The queens emerge from hibernation in the earth early in spring and make their nests a short way underground, furnishing them with large waxy cells in which food is stored and a first brood of workers is reared.

103. BEE-FLY (*Bombylius major*). Known commonly as the 'primrose sprite', this small, furry insect can be seen hovering and darting over many early spring flowers after the manner of a humming-bird hawk moth. It withdraws nectar with its long proboscis while touching down lightly on the flowers. The larvae are parasitic in the nests of various mining bees, first consuming stores and then the bee grubs.

104. ADDER or VIPER (*Vipera berus*). Our only venomous snake, very variable in colour, this species is distinguished by the dark zigzag along its back and the thick body tapering to a small head. It is widely distributed on moors, heaths and dunes, but absent from Ireland. Mating occurs in spring and the young are born in June. Rubber boots afford good protection for walkers in adder country.